STAR WARS®

HONOR AND DUTY

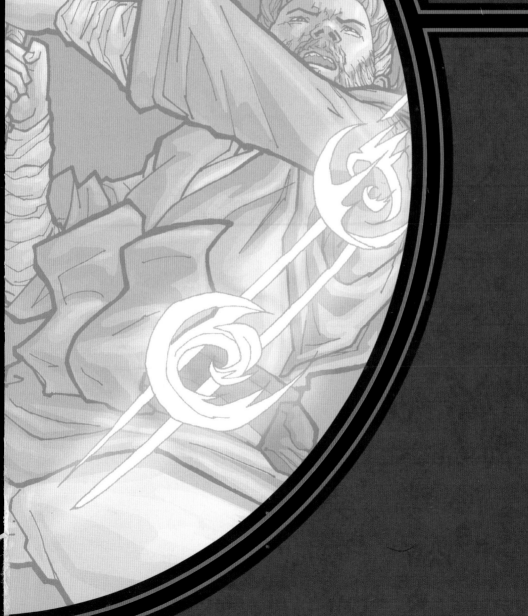

STAR WARS®

HONOR AND DUTY

DARK HORSE BOOKS™

cover illustration by
LUKE ROSS & JASON KEITH

publisher
MIKE RICHARDSON

collection designer
DEBRA BAILEY

assistant editor
DAVE MARSHALL

associate editor
JEREMY BARLOW

editor
RANDY STRADLEY

special thanks to SUE ROSTONI, LELAND CHEE,
and AMY GARY at Lucas Licensing

STAR WARS®: HONOR AND DUTY

This volume collects issues #46 through #48 and #78 of the Dark Horse comic-
book series *Star Wars: Republic*.

Published by
Dark Horse Books
a division of Dark Horse Comics, Inc.
10956 SE Main Street
Milwaukie, OR 97222

www.darkhorse.com
www.starwars.com

To find a comics shop in your area,
call the Comic Shop Locator Service toll-free at 1-888-266-4226

First edition: May 2006
ISBN-10: 1-59307-546-4
ISBN-13: 978-1-59307-546-0

1 3 5 7 9 10 8 6 4 2

PRINTED IN CHINA

Illustration by
STEVE FIRCHOW

Approximately three years before the events in *Revenge of the Sith* . . .

script by
JOHN OSTRANDER

pencils by
C. P. SMITH

inks by
JASEN RODRIGUEZ

colors and letters by
BRAD ANDERSON & JOE WAYNE

CORUSCANT, CITY PLANET AND GOVERNMENTAL CENTER OF THE REPUBLIC, EIGHT YEARS AFTER THE BATTLE OF NABOO...

SOME HOURS LATER...

WORST ANTIGRAV PILE-UP I'VE EVER SEEN. TWENTY DEAD, MAYBE MORE...

THE ACCIDENTS WERE TRIGGERED BY A FALLING BODY, *SAGORO*.

SO?

TERRIBLE THING. BUT HOW DOES IT INVOLVE *US*? WE'RE *SENATE GUARDS*. WE DON'T HANDLE ACCIDENT REPORTS.

THE DECEASED WAS A *SENATOR*.

IT WASN'T THE FALL THAT KILLED HIM. HE WAS DEAD *BEFORE* HE WAS THROWN OVER THE SIDE. PROBABLY FROM HIS QUARTERS AT 500 REPUBLICA.

THIS GETS *WORSE*, DOESN'T IT?

THE DECEASED IS *JHERAMAHD GREYSHADE*.

AH, SON OF A MURGLAK!

NOW YOU KNOW WHY IT'S A MATTER FOR THE SENATE GUARD.

WITH DUE RESPECT, SUPREME CHANCELLOR, THE PROTECTION OF MEMBERS OF THE SENATE IS THE CHARTER OF THE **SENATE GUARD**. WE DON'T **NEED** JEDI.

NORMALLY, I'D AGREE...

...BUT WE'RE DEALING WITH AN **EXTRAORDINARY** SITUATION AT THE MOMENT. THE **FINANCIAL REFORM ACT** COMES UP FOR A VOTE SOON, AND THE VERY EXISTENCE OF THE REPUBLIC MAY HINGE UPON IT.

SEVERAL SYSTEMS HAVE BECOME FED UP WITH THE BLATANT CORRUPTION IN THE REPUBLIC. UNLESS THE SENATE SHOWS A WILLINGNESS TO FINALLY CORRECT THE ABUSES, I FEAR THESE SYSTEMS MAY **SEPARATE** FROM THE REPUBLIC.

I NOW REPRESENT A NUMBER OF PLANETS-- THE **COMMONALITY**-- AND THEIR VOTES REPRESENT THE **SWING VOTES** IN A BADLY DIVIDED SENATE.

I MYSELF AM NOT YET CERTAIN **WHICH** WAY I WILL VOTE ON THE MATTER.

YOUR LATE **COUSIN** WAS QUITE SURE.

WHICH MAY BE WHAT **KILLED** HIM, SUPREME CHANCELLOR. I INTEND TO LISTEN TO **BOTH** SIDES AND MAKE MY DECISION WHEN I VOTE. **IF** YOU THINK THESE **TWO** JEDI ARE ENOUGH TO KEEP ME FROM GETTING ASSASSINATED BEFORE THEN.

IT WILL BE THE JEDI'S RESPONSIBILITY TO PROTECT SENATOR GREYSHADE.

THE SENATE GUARD WILL INVESTIGATE JHERAMAHD GREYSHADE'S MURDER AND ATTEMPT TO DISCOVER WHOEVER IS BEHIND IT. IS THIS CLEAR?

I DARE SAY YOUNG SKYWALKER COULD DO IT ALONE. I CREDIT HIM WITH A GREAT PART OF THE RESCUE OF NABOO. HE SINGLE-HANDEDLY DESTROYED THE TRADE FEDERATION CONTROL SHIP-- WHEN HE WAS MERELY A BOY.

ALWAYS A *PLEASURE* TO SEE YOU AGAIN, YOUNG SKYWALKER.

THANK YOU, SUPREME CHANCELLOR.

WE SERVE YOUR WILL, SUPREME CHANCELLOR.

GUARDSMAN OMIN. I SENSE THAT THE FORCE IS STRONG WITH YOU...

AUTEM HERE.

DEET DEET

WERE YOU EVER TESTED FOR POTENTIAL AS A JEDI?

YES. HOWEVER, I WAS DEEMED TOO OLD TO BEGIN MY TRAINING--

--I WAS ALREADY TWO-YEARS OF AGE, YOU SEE, AND HAD BONDED WITH MY PARENTS.

I WAS *NINE* WHEN I BECAME A JEDI.

AH. WELL. ACCORDING TO THE SUPREME CHANCELLOR, YOU ARE *EXTRAORDINARY*. I AM MERELY *ORDINARY*, IT SEEMS.

I... I DIDN'T MEAN...

WE'VE GOT TO GO. NOW.

WE SHOULD *COORDINATE* OUR PLANS...

IT'S REAL SIMPLE, JEDI. YOU DO YOUR JOB AND KEEP THE SENATOR ALIVE. WE DO OUR JOB AND FIND OUT WHO'S TRYING TO KILL HIM.

WE CAN COMPARE NOTES LATER.

THAT WAS REMARKABLY RUDE, SAGORO. EVEN FOR YOU.

JEDI GIVE ME A PAIN. THEM AND THEIR FORCE MUMBO-JUMBO. I GOT *OTHER* PROBLEMS. *SULA* CALLED ME.

LET ME GUESS. IT'S **REYMET** AGAIN.

MY IDIOT SON IS OFF WITH THAT FELACAT GIRLFRIEND OF HIS. THEY'RE GARBAGE PIT RACING AND THIS TIME--

--HE'S TAKEN HIS LITTLE SISTER **LISSA** WITH HIM!

SHORTLY...

I DON'T GET IT, ISARU! IT'S AS IF HE **WANTS** TO GET KICKED OUT OF THE GUARDS' ACADEMY! HE'S FOURTH GENERATION GUARDS, BLAST IT!

A LOT TO LIVE UP TO.

WORD IS THE JUDICIALS ARE PLANNING A RAID TO CRACK DOWN ON THE ILLEGAL PIT RACING. LISTEN, ISARU--

--WHY DON'T YOU CHECK ON THE LATE SENATOR'S SERVING DROIDS? I'LL JOIN UP WITH YOU LATER.

NOT A CHANCE. I'M YOUR PARTNER. I'M IN.

BESIDES, BEEN A WHILE SINCE I'VE SEEN SOME FIRST-CLASS GARBAGE PIT DIVERS.

WHERE ARE THEY HOLDING THE RACE **TODAY**?

"YOU FEEL THE SAME ABOUT YOUR DAUGHTER, *LISSA*? NO? I DIDN'T THINK SO."

THIS IS SO BOMBAD!

LISSA ENJOYS HERSELF, YES?

OH *YES, RIAO!* THANKS FOR TAKING ME! I DON'T CARE WHAT MOM AND DAD THINK-- I REALLY *LIKE* YOU! REYMET DOES, TOO. I KNOW.

I KNOW. REYMET TRY HARD MAKE CREDS TO HELP RIAO GO HOME TO FELACAT. HE THINK MAYBE CORUSCANT NOT SO GOOD FOR ME. MAKE ME SICK.

REYMET BEST HEART I FIND SINCE PARENTS DIE. GOOD HEART HIM.

LOOK! BROTHER MAKE BIG MOVE NOW! LISSA WATCH!

NOW, LADIES AND GENTLEMEN, BOYS AND GIRLS, REYMET AUTEM MAKES A BRILLIANT AND BOLD MOVE! NONE BUT HE WOULD BE SO DARING!

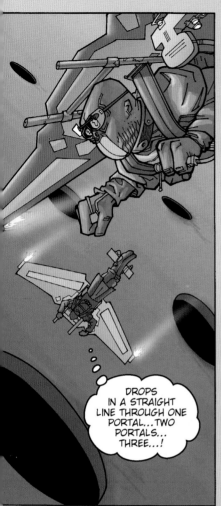

AND HERE COMES THE JUDICIALS!

GREAT. THERE'S MY IDIOT CHILD.

ATTENTION ALL SENTIENTS. THIS IS AN ILLEGAL ACTIVITY BY CODE XT490.6. YOU WILL SURRENDER QUIETLY TO THE PROPER AUTHORITIES NOW MOVING AMONG YOU.

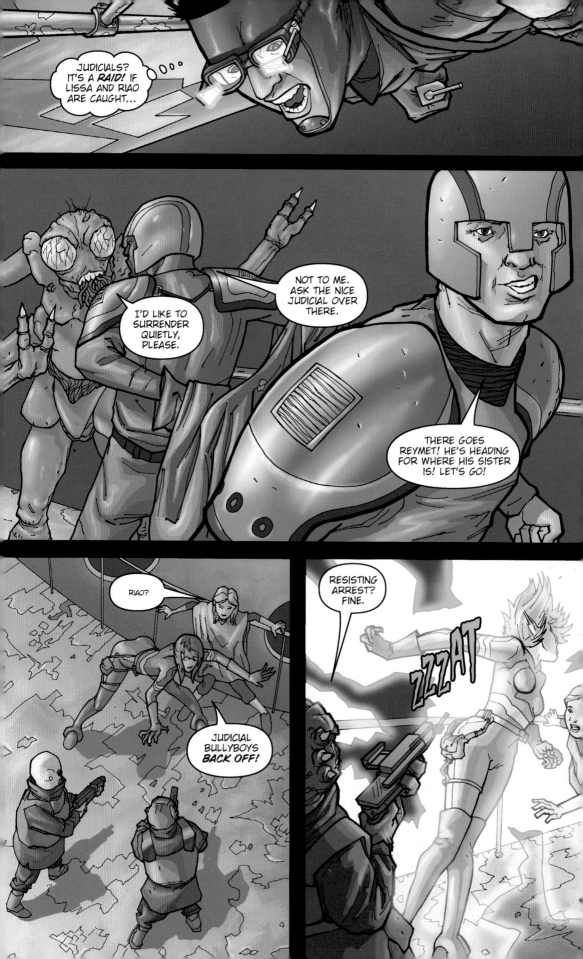

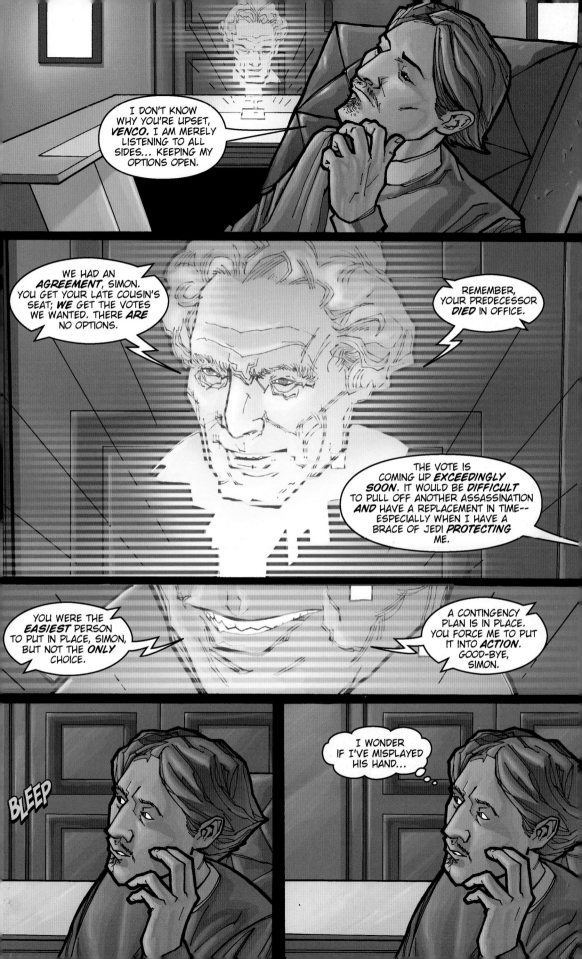

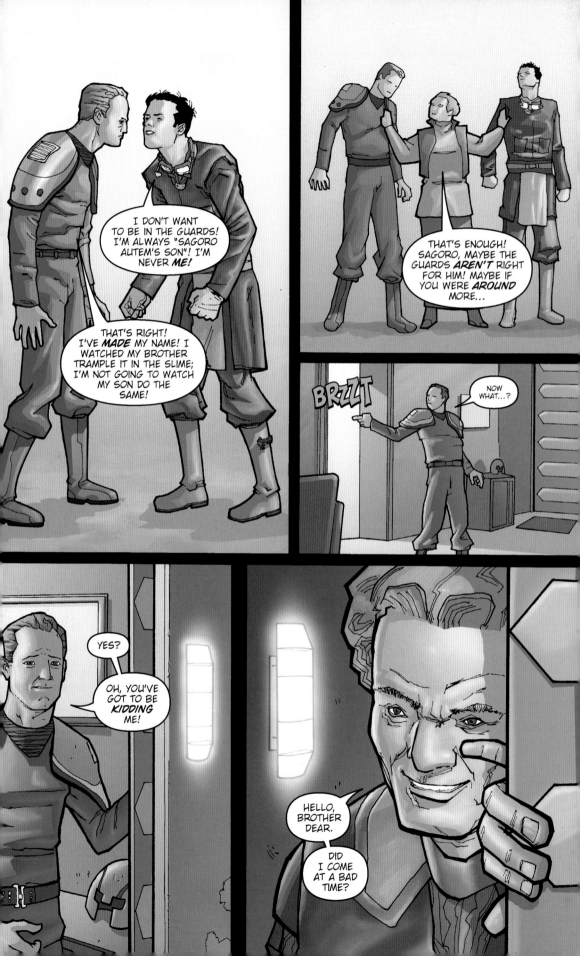

ANAKIN! WHERE IS THE SENATOR?!

HE ASKED TO STEP OUT ONTO THE BALCONY WITH PRINCESS TSIAN, AND I THOUGHT THERE WOULD BE NO HARM IF I STOOD CLOSE BY...

THE SENATE GUARDS JUST WARNED ME THAT SHE MAY BE OUR ASSASSIN!

ZZZZ ZZZZ

YAAAH!

WHAT *ARE* THEY, MASTER?

THEY'RE LIKE THE *CHALLAT EATERS* I FOUGHT MANY YEARS AGO-- SMALL WINGED KNIVES. LIGHTSABERS WILL DO VERY LITTLE GOOD, PADAWAN! USE THE FORCE!

THERE'S TOO MANY OF THEM, MASTER! WE NEED TO GET HIM INSIDE!

WAIT! PRINCESS TSIAN WAS WITH ME-- WHAT'S HAPPENED TO HER?!

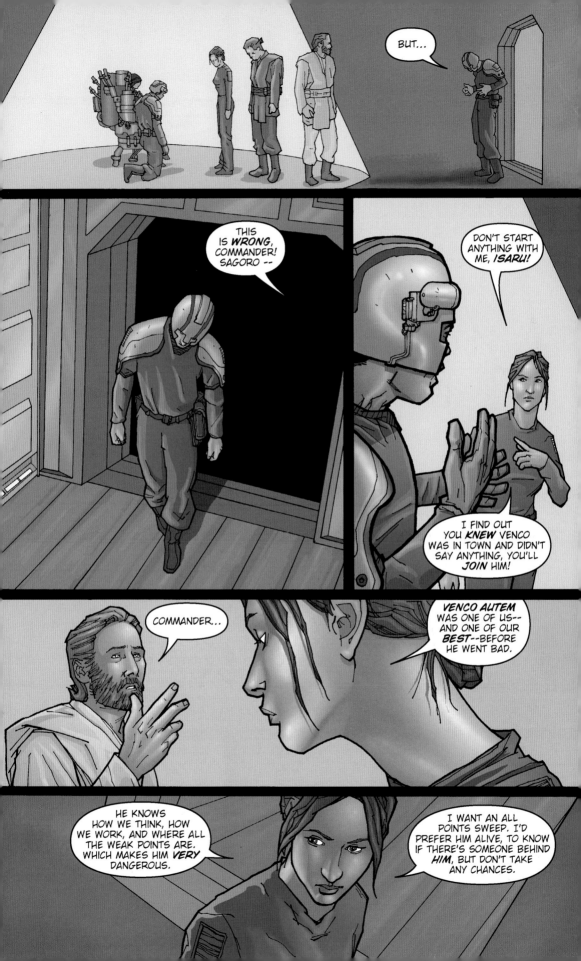

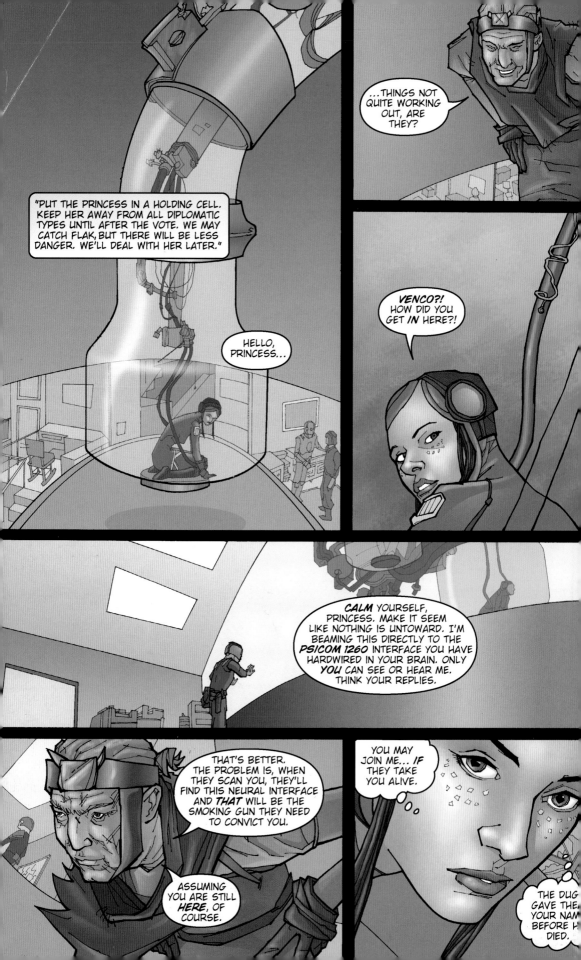

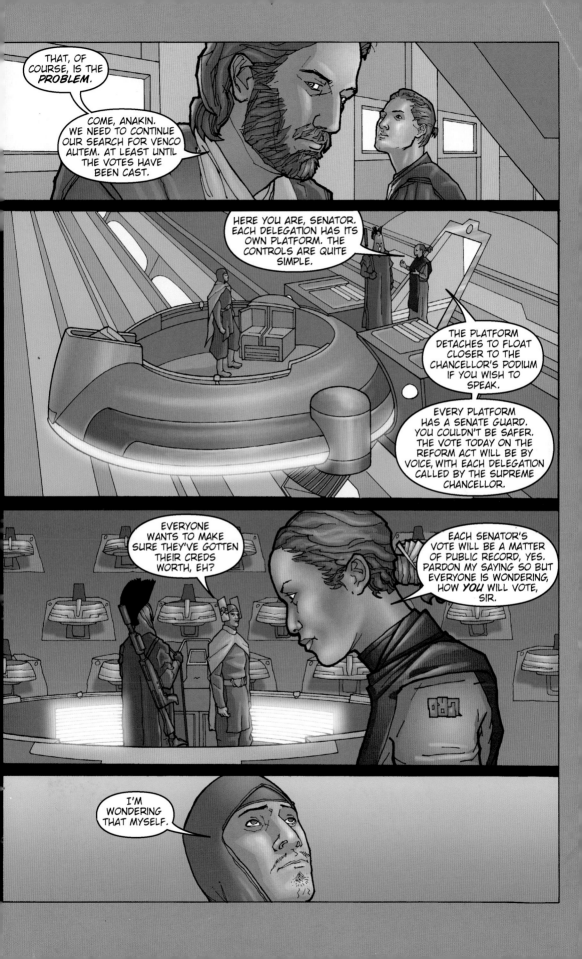

FOOM
FOOM
FOOM

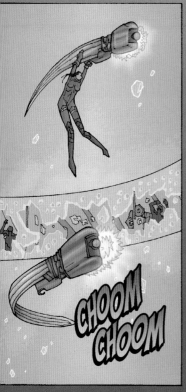

CHOOM
CHOOM

SET ME DOWN HERE!

THIS WAY!

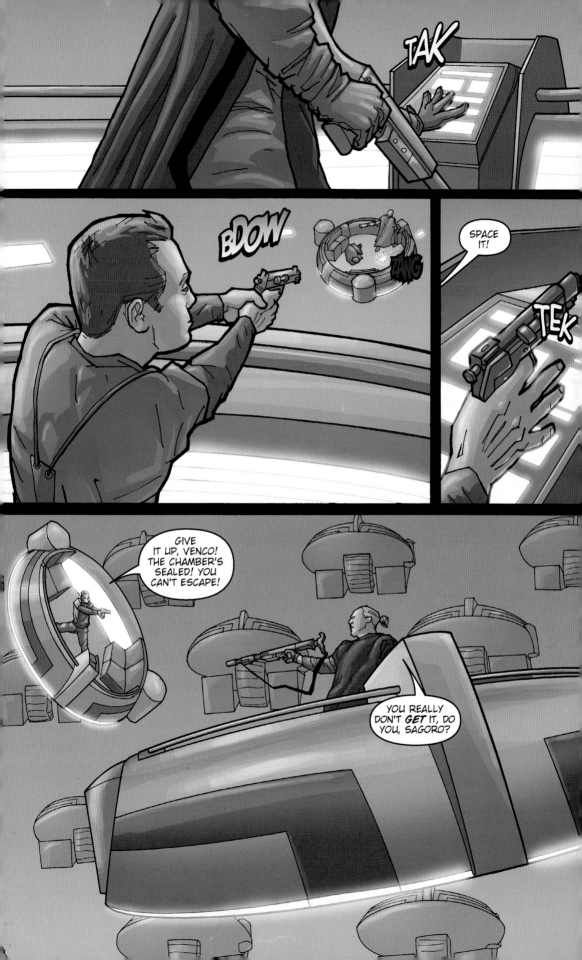

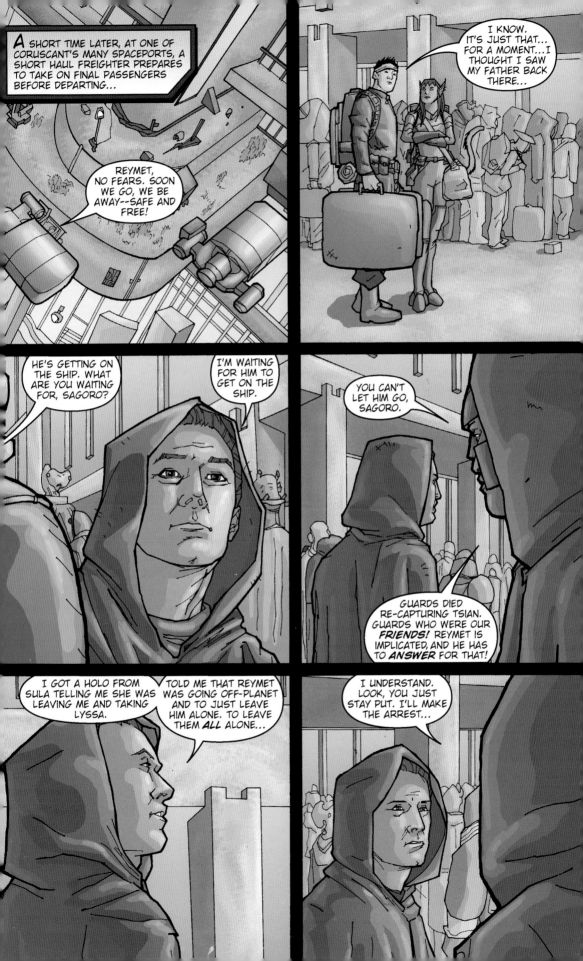

LUKE ROSS & JASON KEITH

Approximately two weeks after the events in *Revenge of the Sith* . . .

script by
JOHN OSTRANDER

pencils by
LUKE ROSS

colors by
JASON KEITH

letters by
MICHAEL DAVID THOMAS

IN THE FIRST DAYS FOLLOWING THE END OF THE CLONE WARS, RUMORS ABOUND ... RUMORS OF *TREACHERY* BY THE JEDI, NECESSITATING THEIR SUDDEN *PURGE* FROM THE GALAXY.

CERTAIN CAPTAINS OF THE NEWLY RE-NAMED *IMPERIAL FLEET* HAVE BEEN SUMMONED TO CORUSCANT. NO EXPLANATION IS FORTHCOMING.

GIVEN THE FATE OF THE JEDI, THERE ARE THOSE WHO ANSWER THE SUMMONS WITH SOME *CAUTION.*

AH! *SAGORO AUTEM,* THE HERO OF SALEUCAMI, I BELIEVE.

UHHN...

AKK...

WHAM!

ARE THERE ANY *OTHERS* WHO QUESTION THE WORD OF THE EMPEROR?

AS OFFICERS OF THE IMPERIAL NAVY, YOUR LOYALTY IS *EXPECTED* ... AND *DEMANDED.*

RESIGNATIONS ARE NOT *PERMITTED* AT THIS TIME. THE GALAXY REMAINS *UNSTABLE.* YOU WILL DO YOUR DUTY OR YOU WILL SHARE THE LATE CAPTAIN DALLIN'S FATE.

EVALUATIONS WILL BE MADE OF YOUR FITNESS FOR COMMAND, GENTLEMEN. LORD VADER WILL KEEP YOU INFORMED OF ANY NECESSARY ... ADJUSTMENTS. DISMISSED.

THIS IS *NOT* WHAT I SIGNED UP FOR, JAN! I NEVER PLANNED TO MAKE THE NAVY MY LIFE'S WORK. I SIGNED UP JUST FOR THE DURATION.

AND THE WAY THAT VADER CHARACTER TREATED DALLIN!

THEY WERE LOOKING TO MAKE AN EXAMPLE AND JACE, UNFORTUNATELY, GAVE THEM A *TARGET.*

ONCE THINGS HAVE QUIETED DOWN, I'M SURE THEY'LL LET THOSE OF US WHO *WANT* TO, LEAVE.

IN THE MEANTIME, BE *CAREFUL* WHAT YOU SAY -- AND TO *WHOM,* SAGORO.

YOU *THINK?*

I'M SERIOUS. THERE ARE SOME WHO ARE VERY *CERTAIN* WHERE THEIR LOYALTIES LIE -- AND IT IS *NOT* WITH THEIR FELLOW OFFICERS!

THAT NIGHT, SAGORO AUTEM STARES OUT THE WINDOW OF HIS RENTED ROOM. HE COULD HAVE BUNKED IN THE OFFICERS' BARRACKS BUT HE FELT THE NEED FOR SOLITUDE.

IT HAS BEEN FIVE YEARS SINCE HE LEFT, BUT HE KNOWS THIS CITY -- THIS PLANET -- WELL. IN THOSE DAYS, HE HAD NO INTEREST IN GOING OFF-WORLD. COULDN'T IMAGINE WHY HE WOULD WANT TO. CORUSCANT HAD EVERYTHING.

BACK THEN, HE'D BEEN A "BLUE" -- ONE OF THE SENATE GUARDS -- AS MEMBERS OF HIS FAMILY HAD BEEN FOR GENERATIONS. AS HE ASSUMED HIS SON WOULD BE.

BUT HIS SON, REYMET, HAD OTHER IDEAS. GOT HIMSELF MIXED UP IN SOME BAD TROUBLE.

SAGORO'S WIFE, SULA, DIDN'T WAIT FOR SAGORO TO CHOOSE BETWEEN FAMILY AND DUTY. SHE TOOK OFF WITH REYMET AND THEIR DAUGHTER LISSA.

SAGORO COVERED THEIR DEPARTURE -- THOUGH IT COST HIM HIS CAREER. AFTERWARDS, HE FLED OFF-WORLD, WORKING AS A MERCENARY, LOOKING FOR HIS FAMILY.

HE FOUND NO TRACE, AND TWO YEARS AGO DODONNA, AN OLD ACQUAINTANCE, CONVINCED HIM TO JOIN THE WAR. THAT SENSE OF DUTY WAS SAID TO BE INBRED IN THE AUTEM FAMILY. WHAT ELSE DID HE HAVE?

SAGORO AUTEM! OPEN UP IN THE NAME OF THE SENATE AND THE EMPIRE!

BAM BAM

SAGORO *AUTEM!* OPEN UP...!

YEAH, YEAH -- I *HEARD* YOU! COMING!

BY THE WAY, IT'S *CAPTAIN* AUTEM...

...WELL, *KARK ME!*

ISARU OMIN.

HELLO TO YOU, TOO, SAGORO.

LET ME COME IN. WE NEED TO TALK.

I THINK WE DID ALL OUR TALKING FIVE YEARS AGO..."PARTNER," WHEN YOU TURNED ME IN FOR LETTING MY SON ESCAPE.

I DID MY DUTY. YOU DIDN'T.

LOOK, I'M HERE FOR A REASON.

YOU NEED TO *HEAR* IT, AND YOU NEED TO HEAR IT *NOW.*

SURE. COME ON IN..."PAL." LET'S RELIVE SOME OF THE OLD DAYS. BACK WHEN WE WERE *PARTNERS.* BACK WHEN WE COULD *DEPEND* ON ONE ANOTHER.

NOT MUCH TIME FOR THAT. THERE'S A SQUAD OF STORMTROOPERS ON THEIR WAY HERE TO *ARREST* YOU, SAGORO.

THERE'S A LIST OF OFFICERS TO BE PURGED FROM THE NAVY, AND YOU'RE ON IT. SENATE GUARD GOT A GLIMPSE OF IT. BELIEVE IT OR NOT, YOU STILL HAVE FRIENDS THERE. I'M ONE OF THEM.

THAT DOESN'T MAKE ANY SENSE!

THEY JUST GOT DONE DECIDING I WAS THE "HERO" OF SALEUCAMI -- WHICH I WASN'T.

I CAN'T TELL YOU *WHY* YOU'RE ON THE LIST. MAYBE YOU'VE SAID SOMETHING YOU SHOULDN'T HAVE -- WOULDN'T BE THE *FIRST TIME* -- OR MAYBE THEY JUST FOUND OUT YOU DID TIME ON BRENTAAL IV.

I JUST KNOW THERE'S A LIST, AND YOU'RE ON IT.

THINGS HAVE *CHANGED* ON CORUSCANT IN THE PAST FIVE YEARS, SAGORO. THINGS HAVE GOTTEN A LOT -- I DON'T KNOW -- *DARKER.*

THEY *GAVE AWAY* THE REPUBLIC WE SERVED. IT'S AN *EMPIRE* NOW. AND THEY CHEERED WHEN THEY DID IT.

)BREEP(CODE FORTY-TWO, ISARU.

YOU'VE GOT TO GO. TROOPERS ARE ABOUT TO ENTER THE HOTEL. HEAD FOR THE ROOF AND OUT.

I'LL STAY HERE AND DELAY THEM AS LONG AS I CAN. I'LL TELL THEM I JUST MISSED YOU.

THIS IS GOING TO CREATE A LOT OF PROBLEMS FOR YOU, ISARU. WHY ARE YOU *DOING* THIS? WE DIDN'T EXACTLY PART ON THE BEST OF TERMS LAST TIME.

MAYBE AFTER ALL THIS TIME I FIGURED OUT WHERE *MY* LOYALTIES SHOULD BE.

NOW GET OUT OF HERE!

I WILL **FIND** THIS SAGORO AUTEM MYSELF, MASTER!

DO NOT MAKE HIM MORE IMPORTANT THAN HE IS, MY FRIEND. AUTEM IS **BENEATH** YOU. SEND **OTHERS** TO FIND HIM.

WE CANNOT TRUST LAW ENFORCE-MENT PERSONNEL, MY LORD. THEY MAY BE **SYMPATHETIC** TO AUTEM.

THEN, LORD VADER, HIRE **BOUNTY HUNTERS.**

IT IS SAID THAT THE HIGHER YOU GO ON CORUSCANT -- THE CLOSER YOU GET TO ACTUAL SUNLIGHT --THE MORE PROMINENT AND IMPORTANT YOU ARE.

NO ONE PROMINENT OR IMPORTANT LIVES ON THIS LEVEL. THE LAST TIME SAGORO CAME HERE, IT WAS THE DOMAIN OF THIEVES, MERCENARIES, SMUGGLERS, INFORMANTS, AND OTHERS OF THAT ILK.

THE PLACE HAS CHANGED SINCE HE WAS HERE LAST. IT'S GROWN MORE **FURTIVE** --

-- MORE **FEARFUL.** THE SECURITY LAWS THAT HAVE BEEN PASSED ARE FELT MORE **KEENLY** HERE.

FEWER SENTIENTS WALK THE STREETS HERE THESE DAYS. THAT MAKES A LONE INDIVIDUAL MORE **NOTICEABLE** -- A QUALITY SAGORO IS TRYING TO **AVOID.**

FORTUNATELY, THE BARS AND CANTINAS ARE STILL OPERATING.

THE LIGHTING IS DIM AND THE PLACE IS CROWDED WITH THE TYPES THAT DON'T WANT TO BE SEEN ON THE STREETS. POTENTIALLY, JUST THE SORT OF SCUM THAT SAGORO NEEDS AT THE MOMENT.

ALL HE HAS TO DO IS SPOT THE *RIGHT* ONE.

IF YOU DIDN'T HAVE THE CREDS, THEN WHY DID YOU CALL ME?

GO AWAY. YOU WASTE MY TIME.

WELL, WELL, WELL. *CH'ORD SY'FON.*

SAGORO AUTEM?!

AREN'T YOU SUPPOSED TO BE...WELL... *DEAD?*

ME? NAW. I'M THE TYPE OF GUY WHO WILL LIVE *FOREVER.* GOT A LONG *MEMORY,* TOO. AND I REMEMBER THAT YOU OWE ME A *FAVOR.*

A QUICK TRIP OFF-PLANET. TONIGHT. NO QUESTIONS ASKED. NO FEE.

JUST BECAUSE WE'RE *PALS* -- YOU AND ME.

VERY WELL. SECTOR 4892, SUB-SECTOR A45B12, PAD 132. THE *SCIMITAR OF KELSO* BOUND FOR NAR SHADDA AT 0300 HOURS.

IT WON'T WAIT.

IT WON'T NEED TO.

PLAY IT STRAIGHT AND WE'RE EVEN. PLAY ME FALSE AND YOU WON'T LIVE TO WORRY ABOUT LOST BUSINESS.

THESE THREE SEEM TO BE THE BEST AMONG THOSE WHO ANSWERED YOUR CALL FOR BOUNTY HUNTERS, LORD VADER.

THE SHISTAVANEN IS NAMED *SEVERIAN*, THE DUG IS CALLED *TARTUTA*, AND THE HUMAN GOES BY *EVAN HESSLER*.

WHY DO YOU WEAR THE MASK, HESSLER?

THE RESULT OF AN "ACCIDENT," LORD VADER.

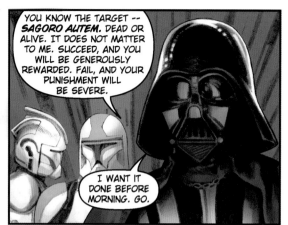

YOU KNOW THE TARGET -- *SAGORO AUTEM.* DEAD OR ALIVE. IT DOES NOT MATTER TO ME. SUCCEED, AND YOU WILL BE GENEROUSLY REWARDED. FAIL, AND YOUR PUNISHMENT WILL BE SEVERE.

I WANT IT DONE BEFORE MORNING. GO.

MY LORD -- A BOTHAN NAMED CH'ORD SY'FON IS WAITING. HE CLAIMS TO HAVE INFORMATION REGARDING AUTEM.

BRING HIM TO *ME.*

THE HOURS DRIFT PAST. SAGORO HAS KEPT TO THE BACK WAYS, LITTLE PATROLLED. 0300 LOOMS AS HE BEGINS TO CAUTIOUSLY MAKE HIS WAY TOWARDS PAD 132.

SAGORO AUTEM! THERE IS A PRICE ON YOUR HEAD. THE *REST* OF YOUR BODY -- NOT SO MUCH.

SURRENDER AND I GIVE VADER BOTH. FIGHT ME -- I TAKE ONLY WHAT I NEED.

HOW YOU WANT TO DO THIS, EH?

UHNN!

?

THAT'S WEIRD. NOBODY ELSE AROUND, THOUGH. ONE OF MY SHOTS MUST'VE GOTTEN HIM AS HE TWISTED AROUND.

I'LL BORROW ONE OF YOUR BLADES, JERK. LITTLE EXTRA INSURANCE IN CASE THERE IS ANYONE ELSE.

BETTER HUSTLE. CH'ORD'S NOT GOING TO HOLD THE SHIP ON ACCOUNT OF ME!

SECTOR 4892, SUBSECTOR A45B12, PAD 132. 0255 HOURS.

RAHHHHR!

OOF!

BACK OFF, BOUNTY HUNTER! YOU COLLECT NOTHING IF YOU'RE *DEAD!*

IT IS PAST THE APPOINTED TIME, AND ALTEM HAS *FAILED* TO APPEAR.

YOU TRY MY *PATIENCE*, BOTHAN.

HE *WILL* BE HERE, LORD VADER! I'M *CERTAIN* OF IT! JUST ... MINUTES...?

NOW SAGORO KNOWS THAT ESCAPE IS NOT A POSSIBILITY. PROBABLY NEVER WAS. ALL THAT'S LEFT IS TO DECIDE WHO KILLS HIM.

I WALK IN AND YOU LOSE THE BOUNTY, RIGHT? HATE TO SEE *THAT* HAPPEN.

BOUNTY'S GOOD FOR ME DEAD OR ALIVE. BETTER MAKE IT DEAD BECAUSE I'M *NOT* GOING QUIET!

OR YOU COULD *WAIT* TEN SECONDS, OLD MAN, AND MAYBE GET A *BETTER* DEAL.

I SWEAR, DAD -- YOU TAKE HARD-NOSED TO A WHOLE NEW LEVEL.

REYMET?!

SHHH! DAD! OR THEY'RE GOING TO *HEAR* YOU AND THIS RESCUE'S GOING TO BECOME A STINKING PILE OF POODOO!

"I'LL EXPLAIN ONCE WE'RE ON *MY* SHIP AND SAFELY OFF CORUSCANT. WE'LL HEAD OUT TOWARDS THE OUTER RIM. MORE ROOM TO MANEUVER, YOU KNOW?"

I'VE BEEN WORKING AS A SMUGGLER AND AN INFORMATION BROKER FOR THE PAST FEW YEARS. BEEN KEEPING UP A NUMBER OF ALIASES. "HESSLER" IS ONE I THINK I'D BETTER LET GO OF.

THE INFORMATION-BROKER THING LET ME KEEP TRACK OF YOU. IT'S HOW I GOT WIND YOU WERE GOING TO BE PURGED. ONCE I HEARD A BOUNTY WAS ON YOUR HEAD --

-- I THOUGHT MAYBE IT WAS TIME FOR A REUNION.

I CAN'T GET OVER YOU. YOU'VE CHANGED. REALLY GROWN UP. LISTEN, DO YOU EVER HEAR FROM YOUR MOM OR YOUR SISTER?

ABSOLUTELY. WE'RE HEADED THERE FIRST. MOM'S NEVER GOTTEN OVER YOU, YOU KNOW. AND LISSA'S DATING A CORELLIAN.

WHAT? WHO TOLD LISSA SHE WAS OLD ENOUGH TO *DATE?!*

"WELCOME BACK, DAD."

END